Preaching

Andrew Fuller (1754–1815)

Andrew Fuller

PREACHING

Foreword by Michael A.G. Haykin

IN PARTNERSHIP WITH

Andrew Fuller
CENTER for BAPTIST STUDIES
at THE SOUTHERN BAPTIST THEOLOGICAL SEMINARY

Preaching

Copyright © 2018 H&E Publishing
www.hesedandemet.com

Scripture taken from the New King James Version®. Copyright © 1982 by Thomas Nelson. Used by permission. All rights reserved. Any Scripture quotations taken from the King James Version will be noted as KJV.

Published by H&E Publishing, Peterborough, Canada
The Andrew Fuller Center for Baptist Studies is under the auspices of The Southern Baptist Theological Seminary, Louisville, Kentucky

Editors: Chance Faulkner and Corey M.K. Hughes
Cover Image: Broadus Chapel at The Southern Baptist Theological Seminary, Louisville, Kentucky

Source in Public Domain: Andrew Fuller, "*Thoughts on Preaching, in Letters to a Young Minister*" and "Preaching Christ" in *The Complete Works of Rev. Andrew Fuller*. Vol II. (Boston: Lincoln, Edmunds & Co, 1833)

First Edition, 2018
Printed in Canada

Paperback ISBN: 978-1-7752633-6-4
Hardcover ISBN: 978-1-989174-03-6
ePub ISBN: 978-1-989174-04-3

CONTENTS

FOREWORD vii
    Michael A.G. Haykin

PREACHING
1. EXPOUNDING THE SCRIPTURES 1

2. SERMONS AND THEIR SUBJECT MATTER 9

3. THE COMPOSITION OF A SERMON 19

4. THE COMPOSITION OF A SERMON 37

5. ON THE ABUSE OF ALLEGORY
   IN PREACHING 43

6. PREACHING CHRIST 49

SCRIPTURE INDEX 59

Publisher's Note

In this edition, the punctuation and capitalization have been modernized, some archaic words have been updated, and a few other slight editorial changes made.

Acknowledgments

Thank you, Michael Haykin for your encouragement in this publication as well as for your help to ensure quality. We also want to thank Ronald Heyboer and Benjamin Inglis for proofreading.

Foreword

Michael A.G. Haykin

Andrew Fuller (1754–1815) is remembered for many things: his defence of the free offer of the gospel and his missional theology, his ardent defence of classical Christianity and keen rebuttal of major theological errors thrown up in the wake of the British Enlightenment (like Deism and Socinianism), the key role that he played as the secretary of the fledgling Baptist Missionary Society from 1793 till his death in 1815, his remarkable ability for sustaining vital Christian friendships with men like

William Carey (1761–1834).¹ Preaching, though, is not something for which he is usually remembered.² Yet, after his official call to the pastoral ministry of Soham Baptist Church in 1775 at the age of twenty-one, there were few Sundays that he did not preach between then and his death forty years later. Possibly one reason why he is often overlooked in surveys of the history of preaching is that, according to his early biographer and one-time friend, John Webster Morris (1763–1836), Fuller

> had none of that easy elocution, none of that graceful fluency, which melts upon the ear, and

---

[1] For the life and ministry of Fuller, see especially Peter J. Morden, *The Life and Thought of Andrew Fuller (1754–1815)* (Milton Keynes, England: Paternoster, 2015). For a briefer study, see Gilbert S. Laws, *Andrew Fuller: Pastor, Theologian, Ropeholder* (London: Carey Press, 1942). Also see the excellent study of "Fullerism" by E.F. Clipsham: "Andrew Fuller and Fullerism: A Study in Evangelical Calvinism", *The Baptist Quarterly*, 20 (1963–1964), 99–114, 146–154, 214–225, 268–276.

[2] There are a few studies of his preaching: see Edwin Charles Dargan, *A History of Preaching* (New York: Hodder & Stoughton/George H. Doran Co., 1912), II, 332–333; Harlice E. Keown, "The Preaching of Andrew Fuller (ThM thesis, Southern Baptist Theological Seminary, 1957); Thomas R. McKibbens, Jr., *The Forgotten Heritage: A Lineage of Great Baptist Preaching* (Macon, GA: Mercer University Press, 1986), 44–52; Paul Brewster, *Andrew Fuller: Model Pastor-Theologian* (Nashville, TN: B&H Publishing, 2010), 110–120; Keith S. Grant, "Plain, Evangelical, and Affectionate: The Preaching of Andrew Fuller (1754–1815)", *Crux*, 48, no.1 (Spring 2012): 12–22; idem, *Andrew Fuller and the Evangelical Renewal of Pastoral Theology* (Eugene, OR: Wipf & Stock, 2013), 77–104.

FOREWORD

captivates the attention of an auditor. His enunciation was laborious and slow; his voice strong and heavy; occasionally plaintive, and capable of an agreeable modulation. He had none of that eloquence which consists in a felicitous selection of terms, or in the harmonious construction of periods; he had a boldness in his manner, a masculine delivery, and great force of expression.[3]

And yet, as Morris admitted, Fuller turned out to be a popular preacher; by the close of his ministry, a thousand or so would regularly attend his preaching in Kettering.[4] More positively, Morris did note that Fuller's "preaching was distinguished for depth of thought, a fulness of scriptural truth, and great perspicacity and force... It was like a blazing torch in the midst of the churches."[5] Fuller also preached in a day when there were a number of pulpit celebrities, including his friends, the seraphic Samuel Pearce (1766-

---

[3] J. W. Morris, *Memoirs of the Life and Writings of the Rev. Andrew Fuller* (London, 1816), 66-67.

[4] Morris, *Memoirs*, 66 and 79.

[5] Morris, *Memoirs*, 82-83. A younger contemporary, Francis Augustus Cox (1783-1853) similarly recalled Fuller as "an extraordinary preacher: plain, practical, judicious, full of rich scriptural illustrations," though "slow and solemn" in his manner of preaching (cited Joseph Belcher in Andrew Gunton Fuller, "Memoir" in *The Complete Works of the Rev. Andrew Fuller*, ed. Joseph Belcher [1845 ed.; repr. Harrisonburg, VA: Sprinkle Publications, 1988], 1:105-107, note *).

1799) and the inimitable Robert Hall, Jr. (1764–1831),[6] the memory of whose preaching overshadowed that of many others like Fuller.

Whatever the reasons for the "forgotten heritage" of Fuller's sermonic corpus,[7] it is evident from various sources, including a large number of extant ordination sermons, that Fuller gave much thought to the significance and nature of preaching in pastoral ministry. The essays in this booklet well reveal the depth of his thinking about preaching, which both he and his Calvinistic Baptist tradition regarded as the preeminent means of grace in the life of Christian communities.

Michael A. G. Haykin, FRHistS
Professor of Church History & Biblical Spirituality,
Director of The Andrew Fuller Center for Baptist Studies,
The Southern Baptist Theological Seminary, Louisville, Kentucky.

---

[6] See the brief discussion of Hall's preaching by McKibbens, Jr., *Forgotten Heritage*, 61–66 and the larger study by Cody Heath McNutt, "The Ministry of Robert Hall, Jr.: The Preacher as Theological Exemplar and Cultural Celebrity" (PhD dissertation, The Southern Baptist Theological Seminary, 2012).

[7] The phrase is that of McKibbens, Jr., *Forgotten Heritage*.

1

EXPOUNDING THE SCRIPTURES

My dear brother,

As you have expressed a wish for a few of my thoughts on your principal work as a Christian minister, I will endeavour to comply with your request, persuaded that what I write will be read with candor and seriousness. The work in which you are engaged is of great importance. To declare the whole counsel of God in such a way as to save yourself and them that hear you[8]—or, if they are not saved, to be pure from their blood—is no small matter. The character of the preaching in an age contributes, more than most other things, to give a character to the Christians of that age. A great and solemn trust therefore is reposed in us, of which we must shortly give an account.

---

[8] 1 Timothy 4:16.

Preaching

The work of a Christian minister, as it respects the pulpit, may be distinguished into two general branches; namely, expounding the Scriptures, and discoursing on divine subjects. In this letter I shall offer a few remarks on the former.

I have found it not a little useful, both to myself and to the people, to appropriate one part of every Lord's day to the exposition of a chapter, or part of a chapter, in the sacred writings. In this way, during the last eighteen years, I have gone over the greater part of the Old Testament, and some books in the New.

It is advantageous to a minister to feel himself necessitated to understand every part of Scripture, in order to explain it to the people. It is also advantageous to a people that what they hear should come directly from the Word of God, and that they should be led to see the scope and connection of the sacred writers. When this is missing,[9] a great number of Scripture passages are misunderstood and misapplied. In going over a book, I have been struck with surprise in meeting with texts which, as they had always occurred to me, I had understood in a sense utterly foreign from what manifestly appeared to be their meaning when viewed in connection with the context.

---

[9] Original: for want of this.

Expounding the Scriptures

Enter into their true meaning

The great thing necessary for expounding the Scriptures is to enter into their true meaning. We may read them, and talk about them, again and again, without imparting any light concerning them. If the hearer, when you have done, understand no more of that part of Scripture than he did before, your labour is lost.

Yet this is commonly the case with those attempts at expounding which consist of little else than comparing parallel passages, or by the help of a concordance, tracing the use of the same word in other places, going from text to text until both the preacher and the people are wearied and lost. This is troubling the Scriptures rather than expounding them. If I were to open a chest of oranges among my friends, and in order to ascertain their quality, were to hold up one and lay it down; then hold up another, and say, "This is like the last;" then a third, a fourth, a fifth, and so on, till I came to the bottom of the chest, saying of each, "It is like the other;" of what account would it be? The company would doubtless be weary, and had much rather have tasted two or three of them.

The scope of the sacred writers is of greater importance in understanding the Scriptures than the most critical examination of terms, or the most labourious comparison of the use of them in different places. When not[10] attending to this, not only particular

---

[10] Original: For want of attending.

passages, but whole chapters, are frequently misunderstood. The reasonings of both Christ and his apostles frequently proceed, not upon what is true in fact, but merely in the estimation of the parties addressed; that is to say, they reason with them on their own principles. It was not true that Simon the Pharisee[11] was a little sinner, nor a forgiven sinner, nor that he loved Christ a little; but he thought thus of himself, and upon these principles Christ reasoned with him. It was not true that the Pharisees were just men, and needed no repentance; but such were their thoughts of themselves, and Christ suggested that therefore they had no need of him; for that he came "not to call the righteous, but sinners to repentance" (Luke 5:32).

Finally, it was not true that the Pharisees who murmured at Christ's receiving publicans and sinners had never, like the ninety-nine sheep in the wilderness, gone astray; nor that, like the elder son, they had served God, and never at any time transgressed his commandment; nor that all which God had was theirs, but such were their own views and Christ reasons with them accordingly. It is as if he had said, "Be it so that you are righteous and happy; yet why should you murmur at the return of these poor sinners?" Now, to mistake the principle on which such reasonings proceed, is to lose all the benefit of them, and to fall into many errors.

---

[11] Luke 7:36–49.

Expounding the Scriptures

Drink into the spirit of the writers

Moreover, to enter into the true meaning of the Scriptures, it is absolutely necessary that we drink into the spirit of the writers. This is the greatest of all accomplishments. I do not mean that you are to expect a spirit of extraordinary inspiration; but that of power, and of love, and of a sound mind. It is impossible to enter into the sentiments of any great writer without a kindred mind. Who but a Pope, or a Cowper, could have translated Homer?[12] And who can explain the oracles of God, but he who, in a measure, drinks into the same spirit? Every Christian knows by experience that, in a spiritual frame of mind, he can understand more of the Scriptures in an hour than he can at other times, with the utmost application, in a week. It is by an unction from the Holy One that we know all things.

I may add, there are some things which, when known, wonderfully facilitate the knowledge of other things. It is thus that a view of the glory of the divine character and government opens the door to the whole mystery of redemption. It is thus also that a lively faith in the sufferings of Christ, and the glory arising out of them, is a key which unlocks a large part of the sacred oracles. While the disciples remained ignorant of his death, they knew but little of the Scriptures, but having learned the design of this great event, a flood of light poured in upon

---

[12] Alexander Pope (1688–1744). William Cowper (1731–1800).

them, and the Old Testament became plain and deeply interesting.

A humble sense of our own ignorance, and of our entire dependence upon God, has also a great influence on our coming at the true meaning of his Word. There are few things which tend more to blind the mind than a conceit of our own powers. Hence we perceive the justness of such language as the following:

> And if anyone thinks that he knows anything, he knows nothing yet as he ought to know (1 Cor. 8:2);

> If anyone among you seems to be wise in this age, let him become a fool that he may become wise (1 Cor. 3:18).

To understand the Scriptures in such a manner as profitably to expound them, it is necessary to be conversant with them in private, and to mix not only faith, but the prayer of faith, with what we read. There is a great difference between reading the Scriptures as a student, in order to find something to say to the people, and reading them as a Christian, with a view to get good from them to one's own soul. That which is gained in the latter of these ways is, beyond all comparison, of the greatest use, both to ourselves and others. That which we communicate will freeze upon our lips, unless we have first applied it to ourselves; or to use the language of Scripture, "tasted, felt, and handled the word of life" (1 Jn. 1:1).

When I have read a psalm or chapter, which I mean to expound, and have endeavoured to understand it, I have commonly thought it right to consult the best expositors I could obtain, trying and comparing my ideas with theirs. Hereby I have generally obtained some interesting thought which had not occurred to me, and sometimes have seen reason to retract what before appeared to me to be the meaning. But to go first to expositors is to preclude the exercise of your own judgment; and after all, that which is furnished by the labours of another, though equally good in itself, will be far less interesting to us than that which is the result of our own application.

I will only add, that I have found it not a little useful to keep a book in which I write down all my expository notes, which though illegible to others, yet answer two purposes to myself: first, by looking them over before I go into the pulpit, I have a clear understanding of every sentence; and secondly, I can have recourse to them on future occasions.

2

Sermons and Their Subject Matter

Though expounding the Scriptures be an important part of the public work of a minister, yet it is not the whole of it. There is a great variety of subjects, both in doctrinal and practical religion, which require to be illustrated, established, and improved; which cannot be done in an exposition. Discourses of this kind are properly called sermons.

It has been requested that I give my thoughts on this part of preaching more particularly.[13] I will endeavour to do so, by considering what must be the matter and the manner of preaching, if we wish to do good to the souls of men.

---

[13] Original: You request me to give you my thoughts on this part of your work somewhat more particularly.

The subject-matter

Unless the subject-matter of your preaching be truly evangelical, you had better be anything than a minister. When the apostle speaks of a necessity being laid upon him to preach the gospel, he might mean that he was not at liberty to relinquish his work in favour of ease, or honour, or any other worldly object; but he was not bound to preach merely, but to preach that doctrine which had been delivered to him. The same may be said of us; woe to us if we preach not the gospel![14]

It may seem to be a very easy thing, with the Bible in our hands, to learn the truth, clear of all impure mixtures, and to make it the subject of our ministry. But it is not so. We talk much of thinking and judging for ourselves, but who can justly pretend to be free from the influences which surround him, especially in early life? We are insensibly, and almost irresistibly, assimilated by the books we read, and the company with which we associate and the principles current in our age and connections will ordinarily influence our minds. Nor is the danger solely external sources:[15] we are "slow of heart" to believe in a doctrine so holy and divine, and prone to deviate at every point. If therefore, we were wholly to think for ourselves, that were no security for our keeping to the mind of Christ.

---

[14] 1 Corinthians 9:16.
[15] Original: from without.

Sermons and Their Subject

I mention these things, not to deter you from either reading or thinking for yourself but rather to intentionally instill[16] the necessity of prayer for divine guidance, and a close adherence to the Scriptures. Though we must think for ourselves, we must not depend upon ourselves but, as little children, learn at the feet of our Saviour.

If you look over the New Testament, you will find the subject-matter of your preaching briefly yet fully expressed in such language as the following:

Preach *the word* (2 Tim. 4:2);

Preach *the gospel* (Rom. 1:15);

Preach *the gospel* to every creature (Mark 16:15);

Therefore it is written, and thus it was necessary for Christ to suffer, and to rise from the dead the third day, and that *repentance and remission* of sins should be preached in his name, among all nations, beginning at Jerusalem (Luke 24:46–47);

I declare to you *the gospel* which I preached to you, which also you have received, and in which you stand, if you hold fast that word what I preached to you, unless you have believed in vain. For I delivered to you, first of all, that

---

[16] Original: to inculcate the necessity.

which I also received, how that Christ died for our sins according to the Scriptures and that he was buried, and that he rose again on the third day according to the Scriptures (1 Cor. 15:1–3);

We preach *Christ crucified* (1 Cor. 1:23);

I am determined not to know nothing among you but Jesus Christ and him crucified (1 Cor. 2:2);

This is the testimony, that God has given to us eternal life, and this life is in his Son (1 Jn. 5:11);

We are ambassadors for Christ, as though God were pleading through us, we implore you on Christ's behalf, be reconciled to God (2 Cor. 5:20);

For he made him who knew no sin to be sin for us, that we might be made the righteousness of God in Him (2 Cor. 5:21);

I have kept back nothing that was helpful, but have proclaimed it to you, and have taught you publicly, and from house to house, testifying both to the Jews, and also to the Greeks, *repentance toward God, and faith toward our Lord Jesus Christ* (Acts 20:20).

Such, my brother, is the concurrent language of the New Testament. Every one of the foregoing passages contains an epitome of the gospel ministry. You will not expect me to expatiate upon their various connections. I may, however, notice three or four particulars, which follow from them.

The manner of preaching
Errand of importance
In every sermon we should have an errand and one of such importance that if it be received or complied with it will issue in eternal salvation. I say nothing of those preachers who profess to go into the pulpit without an errand and to depend upon the Holy Spirit to furnish them with one at the time. I write not for them, but for such as make a point of thinking before they attempt to preach. Even of these I have heard some who, in studying their texts, have appeared to me to have no other object in view than to find something to say, in order to fill up the time. This is not preaching but merely talking about good things. Such ministers, though they think of something beforehand, yet appear to me to resemble Ahimaaz, who ran without tidings.[17] I have also heard many an ingenious discourse, in which I could not but admire the talents of the preacher but his only object appeared to be to correct the grosser vices, and to form the manners of his audience, so as to render them useful members of civil society. Such ministers have an errand

---

[17] 2 Samuel 18:22.

but not of such importance as to save those who receive it, which sufficiently proves that it is not the gospel.

In preparing for the pulpit, it would be well to reflect in some such manner as this: I am expected to preach, it may be to some hundreds of people, some of whom may come several miles to hear; and what have I to say to them? Is it for me to sit here studying a text merely to find something thing to say to fill up the hour? I may do this without imparting any useful instruction, without commending myself to any man's conscience, and without winning, or even aiming to win, one soul to Christ. It is possible there may be in the audience a poor miserable creature, labouring under the load of a guilty conscience. If he depart without being told how to obtain rest for his soul, what may be the consequence? Or, it may be, some stranger may be there who has never heard the way of salvation in his life. If he should depart without hearing it now, and should die before another opportunity occurs, how shall I meet him at the judgement stand[18] of God? Possibly someone of my constant hearers may die in the following week and is there nothing I should wish to say to him before his departure? It may be that I myself may die before another Lord's day—this may be the last time that I shall ascend the pulpit; and have I no important testimony to leave with the people of my care?

---

[18] Original: at the bar of God.

Every sermon should contain a portion of the doctrine of salvation by the death of Christ
If there be any meaning in the foregoing passages, this is emphatically called the gospel. Therefore a sermon in which this doctrine has not a place, and I might add, a prominent place, cannot be a gospel sermon. It may be ingenious, it may be eloquent; but a lacking of the doctrine of the cross is a defect which no pulpit excellence can supply.

Far be it from me to encourage a nitpicking mood[19] manifested by some hearers, who object to a sermon unless the cross of Christ be the immediate and direct topic of discourse. There is a rich variety in the sacred writings, and so there ought to be in our ministries.[20] There are various important truths supposed by this great doctrine, and these require to be illustrated and established. There are various branches pertaining to it, which require to be distinctly considered. Various consequences arising from it, which require to be pointed out. Various duties corresponding with it, which require to be intentionally taught.[21] And various harmful evils[22] to it, which may require to be exposed. All I mean to say is, that as there is a relation between these subjects and the doctrine of the cross, if we would introduce

---

[19] Original: encourage that fastidious humour manifested.
[20] Original: our ministrations.
[21] Original: to be inculcated.
[22] Original: various evils inimical.

them in a truly evangelical manner, it requires to be in that relation. I may establish the moral character and government of God; the holiness, justice, goodness, and perpetual obligation of the law; the evil of sin; and the exposedness of the sinner to endless punishment; but if I have any other end in view than, by convincing him of his lost condition, to make him feel the need of a Saviour, I cannot be said to have preached the gospel; nor is my reasoning, however forcible, likely to produce any good effect. I may be very pointed in pressing the practical parts of religion, and in reproving the sins of the times; but if I enforce the one, or speak against[23] the other, on any other than evangelical principles, I, in so doing, preach not the gospel. All Scriptural preaching is practical; but when practice is enforced in opposition to doctrine, or even to the neglect of it, it becomes anti-scriptural. The apostolic precept runs thus:

> Preach the Word! Be ready in season and out of season. Convince, rebuke, exhort, with all longsuffering and teaching (2 Tim. 4:2).

We must be heralds of the gospel
In preaching the gospel, we must not imitate the orator, whose attention is taken up with his performance, but rather the herald, whose object is to publish, or proclaim, good tidings. There is in the one an earnestness, a

---

[23] Original: or inveigh another.

fullness of heart, a mind so interested in the subject as to be inattentive to other things, which is not in the other— "We believe, and therefore speak" (2 Cor. 4:13). The emphatical meaning of the terms κηρύσσω, εὐαγγελίζω, to preach, and preach the gospel, is noticeable in the account given of the ministry of John the Baptist: "The law and the prophets were until John. Since that time the kingdom of God has been preached, and everyone is pressing into it" (Luke 16:16). Moses and the prophets spoke of things at a distance but John did more than prophesy—his was "the voice of one that cried;" he announced the fulfillment of what had been foretold, proclaiming the Messiah as being among them, and his kingdom as at hand.[24] He opened the door of salvation, and great numbers pressed in!

Earnest calls, and pressing invitations
Though the doctrine of reconciliation by the blood of Christ forms the groundwork of the gospel embassy, yet it belongs to the work of the ministry, not merely to declare that truth, but to accompany it with earnest calls and pressing invitations to sinners to receive it, together with the most solemn warnings and threatenings to unbelievers who shall continue to reject it.

The preaching of both John and Christ is, indeed, distinguished from the calls to repentance and faith which they addressed to their hearers, as being the

---

[24] John 1:23; Mark 1:3; Isaiah 40:3.

ground on which they rested but the latter were no less essential to their work than the former. John came "preaching in the wilderness of Judea and saying, 'Repent'" (Matt. 3:1-2). After John was put in prison, Jesus came into Galilee, "preaching the gospel of the kingdom of God and saying, 'The time is fulfilled, and the kingdom of God is at hand; repent, and believe the gospel'" (Mark 1:15). And thus the apostle explains the ministry of reconciliation as comprehending not only a declaration of the doctrine, but the persuading of men, "pleading" them to be "reconciled to God" (2 Cor. 5:18-20).

There is nothing in all this which clashes with the most entire dependence on the influence of the Holy Spirit to give success to our ministry. Though we invite men, yet it is not on their pliability that we must rest our hopes, but on the power and promise of God. These are a part of the weapons of our warfare but it is through God that they become mighty to the pulling down of strongholds.

3

THE COMPOSITION OF A SERMON
The Topical Method

You have requested my thoughts on the composition of a sermon. There are several publications on this subject well worthy of your notice. If what I may offer have any peculiar claim to your attention, it will be on account of its familiarity.

The form or manner in which a sermon is composed and delivered is of some importance, inasmuch as it influences the attention, and renders the matter delivered more or less easy of being comprehended and retained.

In general, I do not think a minister of Jesus Christ should aim at fine composition for the pulpit. We ought to use sound speech, and good sense; but if we aspire after great elegance of expression, or become very exact in the formation of our periods, though we may amuse and please the ears of a few, we shall not profit the many, and consequently shall not answer the great end of our ministry. Illiterate hearers may be very poor judges of preaching yet the effect which it produces upon them is the best criterion of its real excellence.

A considerable part of the ministerial gift consists in fruitfulness of invention but that which greatly aids in the composition and delivery of a sermon is spirituality of mind. Without this we shall get no good ourselves, and be likely to do but little good to others. The first thing, therefore before we sit down to study, should be to draw near to God in prayer. Spiritual things are spiritually discerned.

When a passage of Scripture is fixed on as the ground of a sermon, it is necessary to read it in connection with the context, and endeavour by your own judgment to gain a clear idea of its genuine meaning. Having formed your own judgment, I would then advise you to consult expositors, who may throw additional light upon it, or give a different sense to it; and if the sense which they give appear to have evidence in its favour, you must relinquish your own. Be satisfied, at all events, that you have the mind of the Holy Spirit before you proceed.

In the next place, having determined on the meaning of the text, it is necessary to examine the force of each word or term of importance in it. This may be done by examining the use of the same terms in other places of Scripture by the help of a concordance; but

COMPOSITION: TOPICAL

here a good judgment of your own is required, that you may select a few out of the many parallel texts which really illustrate that on which you have fixed. Some of the worst sermons are made out of a concordance, being a mere collection of similar sounds, which instead of throwing light upon the subject, only throw it into confusion.

The force of words or terms of importance may also be examined to great advantage by a judicious use of contrast. Place all the important terms of your text, one at a time, in contrast with other things, or examine to what ideas they stand opposed. For example, let your text be Psalm 145:16, "You open your hand, and satisfy the desire of every living thing." Begin with the term "open"—"You *open* your hand." What an idea does this convey of the paternal goodness of the great Father of his creation! How opposite to the conduct of many of his creatures one to another, whose hands and hearts are shut! What an idea also does it convey of the ease with which the wants of the whole creation are supplied?

Let me pause a moment and think of their wants. What a quantity of vegetable and animal food is daily consumed in one town! What a quantity in a large city like London! What a quantity in a nation; in the whole world! But men do not compose a hundred part of "every living thing!" Oh what innumerable wants throughout all animate nature; in the earth, in the air, in the waters! From where comes their supply? "You *open* your hand," and all are satisfied. And can all these wants be supplied by only the opening of his hand?

What then must sin be, and salvation from it? That is a work of wonderful expense. God opens his hand, and satisfies all creation, but he must purchase the church with his blood! God is all-sufficient as to power in the one case as well as in the other; but there are things relative to his moral conduct which he cannot do—he cannot deny himself.[25] Here lies the great difficulty of salvation. In what a variety of ways are our wants supplied! The earth is fruitful, the air is full of life, the clouds empty themselves upon the earth, the sun pours forth its genial rays, but the operation of all these second causes is only the opening of his hand!

No, further—we look to instruments as well as means. Parents feed us in our childhood, and supply our youthful wants, ways are opened for our future subsistence, connections are formed, which prove sources of comfort, friends are kind in seasons of extremity, supplies are presented from quarters that we never expected. What are all these but the opening of his hand? If his hand were shut, what a world would this be! The heavens brass, the earth iron; famine, pestilence, and death must follow.[26]

Next take up the pronoun "You." You will infer from this, "If *you* open your hand, should I shut mine

---

[25] 2 Timothy 2:13.
[26] Psalm 104:27–29.

COMPOSITION: TOPICAL

against my poor brother?" This important sentiment will properly occupy the place of improvement towards the close of the discourse.

Consider next the term "hand." There is a difference between the hand and the heart. God opens his hand, in the way of providence, towards his worst enemies. He gave Nebuchadnezzar all the kingdoms of the earth.[27] But he opens his heart in the gospel of his Son. This is the better portion of the two. While we are thankful for the one, let us not rest satisfied in it, it is merely a hand portion. Rather let us pray with Jabez to be blessed indeed[28] and that we might have a Joseph's portion; not only the precious things of the earth and the fullness thereof, but "the favor of him who dwelt in the bush!" (Dt. 33:16).

Proceed: "You satisfy the desire." God[29] does not give grudgingly. It seems to be a characteristic of the divine nature, both in the natural and moral world, to raise desires, not with a view to disappoint, but to satisfy them. O what a consoling thought is this! If there be any desires in us which are not satisfied, it is through their being self-created ones, which is our own fault; or through artificial scarcity arising from men's luxury, which is the fault of our species. God raises no desires as our creator but he gives enough to satisfy them; and none as our redeemer and sanctifier but what shall be

---

[27] Daniel 2:37.
[28] 1 Chronicles 4:10.
[29] Original: God, I see.

actually satisfied. O the wonderful munificence[30] of God! "How great is his goodness, and how great is his beauty!" (Zech. 9:17).

Now, having examined the force of every term of importance, by contrasting it with the opposite idea or ideas, you will find yourself in possession of a number of interesting thoughts, which you may consider as so many recruits. And, having noted them down as they occurred, your next business is to arrange them in order, or to give each thought that place in your discourse which it will occupy to the greatest advantage. Many sermons are a mob of ideas. They contain very good sentiments, but they have no object in view; so that the hearer is continually answering the preacher, very true, very true; but what then? What is it you are aiming at? What is this to the purpose? A preacher then, if he would interest a judicious hearer, must have an object at which he aims, and must never lose sight of it throughout his discourse. This is what writers on those subjects call a unity of design and this is a matter of far greater importance than studying well-turned periods, or forming pretty expressions. It is this that nails the attention of an audience. One thing at once is a maxim in common life, by which the greatest men have made the greatest proficiency. Shun therefore, a multiplicity of divisions and subdivisions. He who aims to say everything in a

---

[30] *Munificence* meaning great generosity.

single discourse, in effect says nothing. Avoid making a head or particular of every thought. Unity of design may be preserved consistently with various methods of division; but the thing itself is indispensable to good preaching.

The following reasons have induced me to hold this opinion:

1. The human mind is so formed as to delight in unity. To divide the attention is to weaken, if not destroy it. President Edward's[31] sermons, though in some respects not proper for imitation, yet in this, are worthy of notice. They all hold up some one great leading truth; and that truth is the spirit of his text, and serves for the title of his sermon. Look over the table of contents to his *Thirty-three Sermons*, and you will find the title of each sermon throw an amazing light upon the text. The sentiment expressed in the title he calls the *doctrine* of the text; and all he says is to *illustrate*, *establish*, or *improve* it. It might be of use, if in the composition of sermons, we were to oblige ourselves, to give titles to them. Many of what are called sermons would be found to require three or four titles to answer to their contents; which at once proves that, properly speaking, they are not sermons.

2. It has been said, and I think justly, that *evidence* should constitute the body or substance of every doctrinal discourse. Evidence may be drawn from

---

[31] Jonathan Edwards (1703–1758).

various sources: as Scripture testimony, example, reason;[32] but evidence always implies a leading truth to be proved. Where this is not the case, the preacher gives himself no opportunity of advancing evidence; consequently his sermon, if it may be so called, will be without body, without substance, and will contain nothing that shall leave any strong impression upon a thinking mind. In launching a cannon attack upon a wall, you would not fire them in all directions[33] at random, first at one place and then at another, but direct your whole force against a particular spot. In the one case your labour would be thrown away, in the other you are likely to make an effectual impression.

3. It is greatly assisting to *memory* both with respect to the preacher and the hearer. Memory is exercised by the relation of one thing to another. Were you to attempt to remember seven different objects which bore no manner of relation to each other, such as water, time, wisdom, fruit, contentment, fowls, and revenues, you would find it almost impossible; but take seven objects which, though different in nature, yet possess some point of unity which associates them in the mind, and the work is easy. Therefore, sun, moon, stars, earth, air, fire, and water, are readily remembered, being so many principal parts of the one creation.

---

[32] Original: the reason of things.
[33] Original: In opening a battery against a wall, you would not throw your balls at random.

Composition: Topical

4. I cannot so well satisfy my conscience unless I have some interesting truth to communicate, or some important duty to enforce. When I have been thinking of the approach of the Lord's day, the questions have occurred to my mind: What message have I to deliver to the people of my charge? What important doctrine to establish? What sin to expose? What duty to impart?[34] What case to meet? What acknowledged truth to improve? The method frequently used seems to afford an answer to none of these questions; but is rather saying, "None at all, only I have a text of Scripture, on the different parts of which I may say something that will fill up the time."

Divisions are either topical, textual, or compound. The first, or topical method, is to collect all your remarks upon a text, and reduce them to a point, like so many rays of light in a focus. In other words, ask yourself, "What important truth is it that the text contains, and which I feel impressed upon my own mind, and wish to impress upon that of the congregation?" And make this the topic of discourse.

After going over the passage before mentioned, as above, you could be at no loss to determine that the leading sentiment would be—the bounty of providence. This is what the old divines called the doctrine of the text; and, when they printed their discourses, this was the title of them.

---

[34] Original: to inculcate.

But, you may ask, what am I to do with this doctrine when I have found it? Am I to make no divisions, or subdivisions? Of what is my discourse to be composed? Yes, there must be divisions, and perhaps subdivisions; but let them not be so many distinct subjects, which have no relation to each other, but so many parts of a whole. When I have a subject before me, I sometimes ask myself three questions: What is it? On what evidence does it rest? And what does it concern me, or any of the people, if it be true? The division of many subjects will therefore be, 1. Explain the doctrine. 2. Establish it. 3. Improve it.

Let us try the above subject on this plan, and see whether we cannot find a place, under one or other of these heads, for all the foregoing thoughts, which occurred spontaneously on looking over the terms; and perhaps, as we go along, others no less interesting may occur.

Introduction
However men have been in the dark respecting God, it has not been due to a lack of evidence. He is not far from every one of us; for in him we live, and move, and have our being.[35] Creation is full of God.

There is something in this passage wonderfully sublime. It expresses a great truth in the most simple language. It represents the great Creator as the Father of his creation, encompassed round by an innumerable

---

[35] Acts 17:28.

family, whose eyes all wait on him for daily food; while he, with paternal goodness, opens his bounteous hand, and satisfies their various wants.

The subject which invites our attention is—the bounty of providence. In discoursing on it, I shall offer some remarks by the way of explanation—notice the evidence on which it rests—and then improve the subject.

Explanation

Offer some remarks upon the subject by way of explanation. There is much discontent among men. Many objections may arise in the mind to this doctrine, and but few feel themselves duly impressed with its reality. In order to obviate such objections, I would observe:

1. The desires which God satisfies are to be restricted to those of his own creating. Men have a number of artificial, self-created, and sinful desires. These he does not engage to satisfy; but merely those which are purely natural.

2. Though God satisfies the desire of every living thing, yet not all in the same way, but of every creature according to its nature and circumstances. Many of the creatures, like the lily, neither toil nor spin, but receive the bounties of providence ready prepared to their hand but this is not the case with all. It is not thus with man, for though we are forbidden to be inordinately careful, yet we must commonly labour for what we have. It is a

part of the load laid upon us, that by the sweat of the brow we shall eat bread.[36] Nor do I know whether there be more of judgment than of mercy in this sentence. Idleness is certainly a soil on which sin grows to its greatest perfection. Considering what man is, it is a mercy that we have employment. It is among the rich who have nothing to do, and the very poor who will do but little, that wickedness is most prevalent.

3. The text expresses what God does ordinarily, not universally, or in all cases. There are cases of famine; seasons, in which God as it were shuts his hand, on account of the sins of men; and, if he shuts his hand, the heavens become brass, and the earth iron, and millions perish for want of bread. There are also cases more common than famine: great numbers of mankind labour under the hardships of poverty, pine away, and are stricken through, for want of the fruits of the field. But this is one of those evils under which the world groans, owing to the sin of man. If there were no waste or intemperance among one part of mankind, there would be a sufficiency and more than a sufficiency for all.

Evidences

We proceed to notice a few of the evidences by which this important truth is supported.

There are some subjects which are difficult to prove, not from a scarcity, but from a profusion of evidence.

---

[36] Genesis 3:19.

COMPOSITION: TOPICAL

Where this is the case, the difficulty lies in selection. I shall content myself with offering three things to your consideration.

1. The supplies we constantly receive cannot be ascribed to our own labour as their first cause. The whole of human labour is but a kind of manufactory of the materials with which God is pleased to furnish us. We make nothing; we only change the forms of different productions, to suit our convenience. We are as really, though not as sensibly, dependent on God as Israel in the wilderness, who were fed with manna from heaven. To this may be added, when we have laboured to the utmost, it amounts to nothing without a divine blessing upon it. Therefore, all that we possess proceeds from the opening of his hand.

2. A consideration of the number and magnitude of the wants of creatures will convince us that nothing short of the all-sufficiency of God can supply them. What a quantity of vegetable and animal food is required by a single town, for only one day! More for a city; more for a nation; more still for a world; and that for a succession of ages! And what are men, when compared with the whole animate creation? All nature teems with life. The earth, the air, the sea, each swarms with being. Where can all these be continually supplied, but by him that made them? "You open your hand, and satisfy the desire of every living thing" (Ps. 145:16).

3. If we consider the various ways and means by which our supplies reach us, we shall be convinced of the

truth in question. God does not satisfy our desires immediately, so much as through the medium of second causes; and, though we may be too insensible of that hand which puts all in motion, yet it is no less engaged than if we were supplied by miracle. A concatenation,[37] or chain of causes, is apparent in the works of God. Our food is prepared by a complicated but beautiful machinery. The heavens are made to hear the earth, the earth to hear the corn, the wine, and oil, and the corn, the wine, and the oil to hear the people. What is that tendency of various parts of the creation to satisfy the desires of other parts, but the operation of his hand, who is concerned to uphold and render happy the creatures that he has made? The earth abounds in fertility, and the air with salubrity.[38] The clouds pour forth their waters on the earth, and the sun its genial rays. Fire and hail, snow and winds and seas contribute to our welfare. We inhale life with every breath we breathe. The elements are employed for our sustenance and happiness.

Look we to instruments as well as means? Tender parents have supplied us during our childhood and youth; ways have been opened for our future subsistence; endearing connections have been formed, which have proved a source of much enjoyment; in seasons of difficulty friends have kindly aided us; supplies have

---

[37] *Concatenation* meaning a series of interconnected things or events.
[38] *Salubrity* meaning promotion of health.

COMPOSITION: TOPICAL

arisen from quarters that we never expected: what are these but the openings of his hand?

Improve the subject
There is no divine truth but is of some account, and this will be found not a little fruitful.

1. If such be the bounty of divine providence, under what obligations do we lie! Yet what actual returns have we made for all this goodness? All the return that God requires is a grateful heart: "You shall love the Lord your God with all your heart" (Dt. 6:5; Luke 10:27). But alas, are there not many of you who are this day his enemies? The idea is shocking, that such a God should have an enemy; yet so it is. The worst thing that was said of one of the worst of men was, "He has eaten at my table, and has lifted up his heel against me!" (Ps. 41:9). God has been feeding a generation of vipers; which under the frost of childhood or adversity, seemed to claim his pity, but which under the sunshine of maturer years and prosperous circumstances, do not fail to hiss and spit their venom in his face. These things must all come into account. All God's goodness, and all our abuses of it, will be brought to light at the last day.

2. From this view of the divine beneficence, what encouragement is there to trust in the Lord under all our wants and difficulties! With what ease can he supply our wants! In how many ways, unknown to us, and unexpected by us, can he give a favorable turn to our affairs:

Trust in the Lord and do good; dwell in the land, and feed on His faithfulness (Ps. 37:3);

The young lions lack and suffer hunger; but those who seek the Lord shall not lack any good thing (Ps. 34:10).

3. If such be the bounty of providence, what is that of grace? If this be the opening of his hand, that is the opening of his heart. If he satisfies natural desires, much more those that are spiritual. That which is only done generally in the one case is done universally in the other. Not one soul shall perish through famine, or any kind of lacking, whose desires terminate on Christ.

Therefore while we cherish gratitude for temporal mercies, let us not rest satisfied in them. God gave Nebuchadnezzar all the kingdoms of the earth.[39] See how light he makes of worldly good, to bestow it on the basest of men; to throw it away, as it were, on his worst enemies. Do not be content with Nebuchadnezzar's portion; but rather covet, with Jabez, to be blessed indeed. Worldly good, though a blessing in itself, is capable of being turned by sin into a curse. Covet the crowning point of Joseph's portion; not only the precious things of the earth, and the fullness thereof; but "the goodwill of him that dwelt in the bush!" (Dt. 33:16, KJV).

---

[39] Daniel 5:18.

Composition: Topical

4. If God be thus good, what must sin be, that can induce him to load this world with such a degree of misery!

5. If God can with such ease supply all creation, what a blessing must redemption be! For the one he has only to open his hand, and the work is done. The other must be accomplished by the purchase of his blood. God was sufficient for the latter, as well as for the former, as to power; but there are things relative to his moral conduct which he cannot do—He cannot deny himself.[40] Here lies the great difficulty of salvation.

6. What a motive is here to be kind to the poor and needy! If we be children of God we must imitate him: "You shall open your hand wide to your brother, to your poor and your needy, in your land" (Dt. 15:11).

This may serve as an example of the topical method of preaching; and where it can be accomplished, it is very interesting. But there are some texts which cannot be easily reduced to a single topic, and indeed it is better not to be confined to one method, but to indulge variety. Whatever method may be pursued consistent with a unity of design is very allowable. This object may be attained in what is called the textual method of division, on which I shall next proceed to offer a few observations.

---

[40] 2 Timothy 2:13.

4

THE COMPOSITION OF A SERMON

The Textual Method

Endeavour to understand a subject before you speak of it. Do not overload your memory with words. Write down a few leading things for the sake of arrangement and assistance of memory; but not a great deal. Memory must not be overburdened. Never carry what you write into the pulpit. Avoid vulgar expressions—do not affect finical[41] ones, nor words out of common use. As to division and arrangement, it barely respects the assortment of your materials. You must endeavour to understand and feel your subject, or the manner in which you divide it will signify but little. But if both these may be taken for granted, then I should say much depends, as to your being heard with pleasure and profit, on a proper discussion and management of the subject.

---

[41] *Finical* meaning finicky.

At all events, avoid a multiplying of heads and particulars. A few well-chosen thoughts, matured, proved, and improved, are abundantly more acceptable than when the whole is chopped, as it were, into mincemeat. It is very common to divide in a textual way, i.e. to propose to discourse first upon one part or branch of it; secondly, upon another, etc. As for example:

In your light we shall see light (Ps. 36:9).

First, inquire what is meant by that light which is ascribed to God—"Your light." Secondly, what is that light which we see in God's light. Thirdly, what is included in seeing this light. I cannot say I approve of this method. It is not, properly speaking, a sermon. A sermon is a discourse on some divine subject, or a train of interesting thoughts on some sacred theme. The above process, I think, should be brought into the introduction and explication of the text, and should be done in about five minutes. Then, having made the text plain by explaining the difficult parts of it, I should state the leading truth taught in the text as the subject or theme of the discourse. For example:

In your light we shall see light (Ps. 36:9).

There is a great boast of light in the world, and there is some ground for it in natural things; but, as of old the world by wisdom knew not God, so of late. If ever we know God, it must be through the medium of his Word. This I take to be the meaning of the passage I have read. The term light in the last clause means the true knowledge of God, and in the first, the true medium of attaining it, namely, divine revelation. The sun seems to amount to this: the Word of God is the grand medium by which we can attain a true and saving knowledge of God. What the sun and stars are to the regions of matter, that revelation is to the mental region.[42] Let us try to illustrate this important truth by a few observations:

1. The knowledge of God was objectively manifested by the light of nature, but through man's depravity rendered inoperative.[43] It is the revelation of the law of the Lord that converts the soul.[44]

2. The true knowledge of God was obtained under the patriarchal or Mosaic dispensation by great numbers, but it was through the medium of revelation. As revelation increased, the knowledge of God increased with it; prophecies, promises, and precepts; types, and shadows. In this light they saw light, though not so clearly as in after days.

3. The true knowledge of God has obtained still more ground under the gospel dispensation; but it is still through the medium of revelation. Whenever the latter has gone among the Gentiles, the former has gone along

---

[42] Genesis 1:13, 17.
[43] Romans 1:28.
[44] Psalm 19:1–11.

with it: and, as revelation is more perfect, God has the more honored it.

4. The light of the gospel dispensation is not yet perfect[45] but, whatever degree of brilliancy arises, it will be through this medium. We must not think we have exhausted Scripture knowledge—we know but little of it yet. A thousand promises and prophecies will appear in a glory, of which we have now but faint ideas. Let us now endeavour to improve the subject.

Endeavour to improve the subject

1. Be thankful for the light of revelation. Regard not the ignis fatuus[46] which wanders about under the name of reason in modern productions.[47]

2. Walk in it particularly in finding your way to eternal life; for settling disputed principles, and regulating your lives.

3. There are many things of which you may entertain no doubt, concerning which there may be no manner of dispute; yet make a point of seeing them in God's light. Many content themselves with seeing them in the light in which great and good men have placed them; but, though angels, they are not the true light: they all view things partially. If what they say be true, yet, if we receive it merely on their representation, our faith will stand in the wisdom of men, and not in the power of

---

[45] Isaiah 30:26.
[46] *Ignis fatuus* meaning something deceptive or deluding.
[47] 2 Peter 1:19.

God.[48] That knowledge or faith which has not God's Word for its ground will not stand the day of trial.

4. Endeavour to spread it in your connections and in the world at large. I do not pretend to say that sermons should be formed after this or any other mode. Every subject, in some degree, requires a mode of discussion for itself. There are however some general observations that will ordinarily apply to most subjects. In doctrinal subjects, in which some great truth is taught, your business is to find out that truth, and state it in the introduction. If clearly stated, search for the evidences, and make it one head of the discourse to establish it. If it be a truth to be illustrated, set it before the hearers in various points of light; and as no divine truth is merely speculative, but some way or other concerns the hearers, the latter part of the subject should consist in improvement. 1. To explain, 2. To establish, 3. To improve it.

But in all cases the division must be governed by the materials you have to divide. It would be absurd to explain a subject that was already as plain as you could make it, or in which there appeared no difficulties or liability to misunderstand. There are three questions I have often put to myself in thinking on a subject—What? Why? What then? In other words—What am I going to teach? Why? Or on what ground do I advance it as a

---

[48] 1 Corinthians 2:9.

truth? And what does it concern any or all of my hearers if it be true?

On practical subjects there is seldom much room for you to prove and improve. Not the former, since there is no truth to be established; not the latter, because the whole sermon is an address upon those things of which no improvement is made. I have generally found that exhortations include matter for a two-fold division, and have very commonly proposed, first, to inquire into the meaning and extent of the exhortation; secondly, to enforce it. Under the former there is room to expatiate[49] upon every idea or branch of the duty. In the latter, to introduce any motive that serves either for that or other texts.

---

[49] *Expatiate* meaning to speak or write at length or in detail.

5

On the Abuse of Allegory in Preaching

After what several able writers have produced of late years upon this practice, particularly the late Dr. Stennett[50] on the Parable of the Sower, it might have been expected that this evil would at least have been considerably diminished. But the misfortune is, those who are most addicted to this way of preaching seem in general to have very little inclination to read. Whether they deem it unlawful, as involving them in the sin charged upon the prophets, of stealing everyone from his neighbour—or whether they be so enamored of their own thoughts as to set all others at defiance—I cannot decide; but certain it is that many preach as if they had never read or thought upon the subject.

Very little observation will convince us that the preachers with whom this practice mostly prevails are of

---

[50] Samuel Stennett (1727–1795).

the lower sort with respect to seriousness and good sense, however high they may affect to soar in their notions. Of such characters I have but little hope. But as some godly men are, I believe, too much infected with this disease, if the editor will indulge me with two or three pages, I will expostulate with one of them on the *cause* and *consequences* of his conduct.

Let me entreat you then, my friend, to consider, in the first place, whether, when you turn plain historical facts into allegory, you treat the Word of God with becoming reverence. Can you seriously think the Scriptures to be a book of riddles and conundrums, and that a Christian minister is properly employed in giving scope to his fancy, in order to discover their solution? I have been asked the meaning of certain passages of Scripture; and when I have answered according to what appeared to be the scope of the sacred writer, it has been said, "Yes, that may be the literal meaning; but what is the spiritual meaning of it?" as though every part of Scripture had a spiritual, that is, a hidden or allegorical meaning, besides its obvious one. That some parts of Scripture are allegorical—that some prophecies have a double reference—and that the principle suggested by many a passage may be applied to other things besides what is immediately intended—there is no doubt—but this is very different from the practice to which I allude. All Scripture is profitable in some way; some for doctrine, some for reproof, some for correction, and

ABUSE OF ALLEGORY

some for instruction in righteousness[51] but all is not to be turned into allegory. If we must play, let it be with things of less consequence than the Word of the eternal God!

Secondly, consider whether the motive that stimulates you to such a manner of treating the sacred oracles be any other than vanity. If you preached to a people possessed of anything like good sense, they would consider it as perverting the Word of God, and whipping it into froth. Instead of applauding you, they would be unable to endure it. But, if your people be ignorant, such things will please them; and they may gaze, and admire, and smile, and say one to another, it may be in your hearing too, "Well, what a man! Who would have thought that he would have found so much gospel in that text? Ah, very true, who indeed?" But what would the apostle Paul say? "Are you not carnal?" Is it for a man of God to "court a grin when he should woo a soul?" For shame desist from such folly, or lay aside the Christian ministry! You are commanded to "shepherd the flock of God, which he has purchased with his own blood,"[52] but it is not everything pleasing to a people that feeds them in the sense of the apostle. He did not mean to direct the Ephesian elders to feed men's fancies, and still less their prejudices; but their spiritual desires, and this is accomplished only by administering to them the words of truth and soberness. If your preaching be such as God

---

[51] 2 Timothy 3:16.
[52] Acts 20:28.

approves, and if you study to show yourself approved of him, it will lead the people to admire your Saviour rather than you, and render him the topic of their conversation.

Thirdly, consider whether both you and your people be not in danger of mistaking this spiritualizing passion for spirituality of mind and a being led into "the deep things of God." There are few objects at a greater distance than the enthusiasm[53] of a vain imagination and that holy and humble spirit by which spiritual things are discerned; yet the one is often mistaken for the other. The preacher dreams of deep discoveries and the people wonder to hear them but what says the Scriptures?—"The prophet that has only a dream must tell his dream; but he that has God's Word, let him speak it faithfully: for what is the chaff to the wheat?" (Jer. 23:28).

Finally, consider the consequences which must follow from this practice. If an unbeliever comes into your assembly, and finds you arraying Christianity in this fancy dress, is it likely he should be convinced of all—and, the secrets of his heart being made manifest, fall down and worship God, and report that God is among you, and that of a truth? If he hears you treat the historical parts of Scripture as meaning something very different from what they appear to mean, will he not say you are mad, and be furnished with a handle for representing religion itself as void of truth and good sense? Or if he hears you interpret the miracles, which

---

[53] Original: than the effervescence.

Abuse of Allegory

Christ wrought in proof of his Messiahship, of that change which is now wrought in the minds of sinners by the Spirit of God, will he not say that you yourselves appear to consider the whole as a string of fables, and are employed in finding out the morals of them?

But perhaps you are seldom attended by men of this description. Be it so; what, do you think,[54] must be the effect of such preaching on professing Christians, either nominal or real? The former will either fall asleep under it, as something which does not concern them; or, if they attend to you, and understand your interpretations, they will think they are quite in the secret, and set themselves down for deep Christians; when in truth, they know nothing yet as they ought to know. And as to real Christians, their souls will either pine under your ministry, or by contracting a false taste, will thirst after the froth of human fancy, to the neglect of the sincere milk of the Word; and instead of growing in grace, and in the knowledge of our Lord Jesus Christ, will make no progress in either.

It is an easy thing for a man of a luxuriant imagination, unencumbered by judgment, to make anything he pleases of the Scriptures, as well as any other book; but in so doing he must destroy their simplicity, and of course their efficacy; which in fact is reducing them to nothing. If they be not applied to their appropriate uses, they are perverted; and a perverted

---

[54] Original text: what think you.

good proves the greatest of evils. Thus it is that characters abound who are full of Scripture language, while yet they are awfully destitute of Scripture knowledge, or Scriptural religion.

6

PREACHING CHRIST[55]

"We preach not ourselves, but Christ Jesus the Lord; and ourselves your servants for Jesus' sake" (2 Cor. 4:5).

A remark, which I once heard from the lips of that great and good man, the late Mr. Abraham Booth,[56] has often recurred to my recollection. "I fear," said he, "there will be found a larger proportion of wicked ministers than of any other order of professing Christians!" It did not appear to me at the time, nor has it ever appeared since, that this remark proceeded from a want of charity, but rather from a deep knowledge of the nature of

---

[55] This sermon given by Andrew Fuller does not originally appear in his work on Preaching. It has been added by the editors.

[56] Abraham Booth (1734–1806).

Preaching

Christianity, and an impartial observation of men and things. It is right for us,[57] not only as professing Christians, but as ministers, to "examine ourselves, whether we be in the faith" (2 Cor. 13:5). It certainly is possible, after we have preached to others, that we ourselves should be cast away! I believe it is very common for the personal religion of a minister to be taken for granted; and this may prove a temptation to him to take it for granted too. Ministers, being wholly devoted to the service of God, are supposed to have considerable advantages for spiritual improvement. These they certainly have; and if their minds be spiritual, they may be expected to make greater proficiency in the divine life than their brethren. But it should be remembered, that if they are not spiritual, those things which would otherwise be a help would prove a hinderance.

If we study divine subjects merely as ministers, they will produce no salutary effect. We may converse with the most impressive truths, as soldiers and surgeons do with blood, until they cease to make any impression upon us. We must meditate on these things as Christians, first feeding our own souls upon them, and then imparting that which we have believed and felt to others; or whatever good we may do to them, we shall receive none ourselves. Unless we mix faith with what we preach, as well as with what we hear, the Word will not

---

[57] Original: it behoves us.

profit us. It may be on these accounts that ministers, while employed in watching over others, are so solemnly warned against neglecting themselves:

> Take heed to yourselves and to all the flock (Acts 20:28);

> Take heed to yourself and to the doctrine. Continue in them, for in doing this you shall both save yourself and those who hear you (1 Tim. 4:16).

Preaching the gospel is not the only work of a Christian minister; but it is a very important part of his duty, and that which, if rightly attended to, will be followed by other things. To this, therefore, I shall request your attention.

You cannot have a better model than that which is here held up to you. The example of the apostles and early church ministers[58] is for our imitation. Three things are here presented to our notice: 1. What they did not preach, 2. what they did preach, and 3. what they considered themselves.

What the apostles did not preach
"We preach not ourselves." It might be thought that this negative was almost unnecessary; for except a few gross impostors, who would ever think of holding up

---

[58] Original: apostles and primitive ministers.

themselves as saviours, instead of Christ? "Was Paul crucified for you? or were you baptized into the name of Paul?" (1 Cor. 1:13). Very true, in this gross sense, few men in the present day will be found to preach themselves. But self may be an object of preaching without being expressly avowed, and even while with the tongue Christ is recommended. And there is little doubt that self is the great end of numbers who engage in the Christian ministry. For example:

1. If worldly advantage be our object, we preach ourselves. It is true there is but little food for this appetite in our congregations. Yet there are cases where it is otherwise. Men have made their fortunes by preaching. And if this has been their object, they have had their reward. If this had not been a possible case, Paul would not have disavowed it as he does: "Not for a cloak of covetousness, God is witness" (1 Thess. 2:5).

2. If we make the ministry subservient to a life of ease and indolence, we preach ourselves rather than Christ. We may get but little for our labour, and yet, being fond of a life of sloth, (if a life it can be called), it may be more agreeable to us than any other pursuit. It is from this disposition that many ministers have got into the habit of spending a large part of every week in gossiping from house to house; not promoting the spiritual good of the people, but merely indulging themselves in idle talk.[59] I might add, it is from this

---

[59] 1 Timothy 5:13.

disposition and practice that a large proportion of the scandals among ministers have arisen. Had there been no danger from these quarters, we should not have met with another of Paul's solemn disavowals: "For our exhortation did not come from error or uncleanness, nor was it in deceit" (1 Thess. 2:3). Such a declaration as this was not without meaning. It describes the false teachers of those times, and of all times.

3. If the applause of our hearers be the governing principle of our discourses, we preach ourselves, and not Christ. To be acceptable is necessary to being useful, and an attention to manner with this end in view is very proper; but if the love of fame be our governing principle, our whole ministry will be tainted by it. This subtle poison will penetrate and pervade our exercises, until everyone perceives it, and is sickened by it, except ourselves. It will innate our composition in the study, animate our delivery in the pulpit, and condescend to fish for applause when we have retired. It will even induce us to deal in flattering doctrine, dwelling on what are known to be favourite topics, and avoiding those which are otherwise. It is a great matter to be able to join with the apostle in another of his solemn disavowals: "For neither at any time used we flattering words, as you know,—nor of men sought we glory" (1 Thess. 2:5-6).

4. If our aim be to make proselytes to ourselves, or to our party, rather than converts to Christ, we shall be found to have preached ourselves, and not him. We

certainly have seen much of this species of zeal in our times: "Men speaking perverse things, to draw away disciples after them" (Acts 20:30). Nor do I refer merely to men who would be thought singularly evangelical, and even inspired of God—who are continually holding up themselves as the favourites of heaven and the darlings of providence and denouncing judgments on all who oppose them; and the tenor of whose preaching is to persuade their admirers to consider themselves as the dear children of God, and all who disapprove of them as poor blind creatures, knowing nothing of the gospel. Of them and their followers I can only say, "If any man be ignorant, let him be ignorant" (1 Cor. 14:38). But men who have paid great attention to the Scriptures, and who have preached and written many things on the side of truth, have nevertheless given but too evident proof that the tenor of their labours has been to make proselytes to themselves, or to their party, rather than converts to Christ.

What the apostles did preach

We preach "Christ Jesus the Lord." This is the grand theme of the Christian ministry. But many have so little of the Christian minister about them, that their sermons have scarcely anything to do with Christ. They are mere lengthy moral arguments.[60] And these, forsooth, would

---

[60] Original: mere moral harangues.

fain[61] be thought exclusively the friends of morality and good works! But they know not what good works are, nor do they go the way to promote them. "This is the work of God, that you believe on him whom he has sent" (John 6:29). Preach Christ, or you had better be anything than a preacher. The necessity laid on Paul was not barely to preach, but to preach Christ. "Woe to me if I preach not the gospel!" (1 Cor. 9:16). Some are employed in depreciating Christ. But do you honour him? Some who talk much about him, yet do not preach him, and by their habitual behaviour[62] prove themselves enemies to his cross. If you preach Christ, you need not fear for want of matter. His person and work are rich in fullness. Every divine attribute is seen in him. All the types prefigure him. The prophecies point to him. Every truth bears relation to him. The law itself must be so explained and enforced as to lead to him. Particularly:

1. Exhibit his divinity and glorious character. The New Testament dwells much on his being the Son of God—equal with God. It was this that heightened the gift of him.[63] Hence the efficacy of his blood.[64] Hence the condescension of his obedience, and the dignity of

---

[61] *Fain* meaning pleased or willing under the circumstances.
[62] Original: habitual deportment.
[63] John 3:16.
[64] 1 John 1:7.

his priesthood.[65] Hence the greatness of the sin of rejecting him,[66] and of apostasy.[67]

2. Hold up his atonement and mediation as the only ground of a sinner's hope. It is the work of a Christian minister to beat off self-righteous hope, which is natural to depraved man, and to direct his hearers to the only hope set before them in the gospel. Be not concerned merely to form the manners of your congregation, but bring them to Christ. That will best form their manners. The apostles had no directions short of this: "Repent, and believe the gospel" (Mark 1:15). They never employed themselves in lopping off the branches of sin but laid the axe to the root. Your business with the sins of mankind is to make use of them to convince your hearers of the corruption of their nature, and their need of a radical cure.

3. Hold up the blessings of his salvation for acceptance, even to the chief of sinners: "This is a faithful saying, and worthy of all acceptation, that Christ Jesus came into the world to save sinners, of whom I am chief" (1 Tim. 1:15).

The gospel is a feast, and you are to invite guests. You may have many excuses and refusals. But be you concerned to do as your Lord commands. And when you have done your utmost, there will still be room. Dwell on the freeness, and fullness, and all-sufficiency of his grace,

---

[65] Hebrews 4:14–16.
[66] John 3:18.
[67] Hebrews 10:29.

PREACHING CHRIST

and how welcome even the worst of sinners are, who renouncing all other refuge, flee to him.

4. Preach him as "the Lord," or Lawgiver, of his church, no less than as a Saviour. Christ's offices must not be divided. Taking his yoke, and learning his spirit, are connected with coming to him. Believers are "not without law to God, but under the law to Christ" (1 Cor. 9:21).

The preaching of Christ will answer every end of preaching. This is the doctrine which God owns to conversion, to the leading of awakened sinners to peace, and to the comfort of true Christians. If the doctrine of the cross be no comfort to us, it is a sign we have no right to comfort. This doctrine is calculated to wake up the sluggard,[68] to draw forth every Christian grace, and to recover the backslider.[69] This is the universal remedy for all the moral diseases of all mankind.

In what light the apostles considered themselves

"Your servants for Jesus' sake." Ministers are not the servants of the people in such a sense as implies inferiority, or their having an authority over them. On the contrary, what authority there is on the other side: "Obey those who rule over you" (Heb. 13:17). Nor are ministers the servants of the people in such a sense as to

---

[68] Original: quicken the indolent.
[69] See Andrew Fuller, *Backslider* (Peterborough: H&E Publishing, 2018).

be directed by them what to preach. In these respects one is their Master, even Christ. But ministers are the servants of their people, inasmuch as their whole time and powers require to be devoted to their spiritual advantage—to know them, caution, counsel, reprove, instruct, exhort, admonish, encourage, stimulate, pray, and preach. Study to promote their spiritual interests as individuals, and their prosperity as a people.

Nor should ministers think it too much to lay themselves out in this work. They do it "for Jesus' sake." This was the motive addressed to Peter: "Do you love me?—Feed my sheep. Feed my lambs" (John 21:17).—"Feed the church of God, which he has purchased with his own blood" (Acts 20:28). Let Christ be not only the theme of my remaining ministry, but the exaltation of him and the enlargement of his kingdom the great end of my life! If I forget you, O my Saviour, let my right hand forget; if I do not remember you, let my tongue cleave to the roof my mouth!

Scripture Index

Genesis
- 1:13, 17 39
- 3:19 29

Deuteronomy
- 6:5 32
- 15:11 34
- 33:16 .... 23, 34

2 Samuel
- 18:22 13

1 Chronicles
- 4:10 23

Psalms
- 19:1–11 39
- 34:10 33
- 36:9 38
- 37:3 33
- 41:9 32
- 104:27–29 22
- 145:16 .... 21, 31

Isaiah
- 30:26 39
- 40:3 17

Jeremiah
- 23:28 46

Daniel
- 2:37 22
- 5:18 33

Zechariah
- 9:17 23

Matthew
- 3:1–2 17

Mark
- 1:3 17
- 1:15 .... 17, 55
- 16:15 11

Luke
- 5:32 4
- 7:36–49 4
- 10:27 32
- 16:16 17
- 24:46–47 11

John
- 1:23 17
- 3:16 55
- 3:18 55

John Continued
- 6:29 54
- 21:17 57

Acts
- 17:28 28
- 20:20 12
- 20:28 .... 45, 51, 57
- 20:30 53

Romans
- 1:15 11
- 1:28 39

1 Corinthians
- 1:13 51
- 1:23 12
- 2:2 12
- 2:9 40
- 3:18 6
- 8:2 6
- 9:16 .... 10, 54
- 9:21 56
- 14:38 54
- 15:1–3 12

2 Corinthians
- 4:5 49
- 4:13 16
- 5:18–20 18

5:20 12
5:21 12
13:5 50

1 Thessalonians
- 2:3 52
- 2:5–6 55

1 Timothy
- 1:15 56
- 4:16 .... 1, 51
- 5:13 52

2 Timothy
- 2:13 .... 22, 34
- 3:16 44
- 4:2 .... 11, 16

Hebrews
- 4:14–16 55
- 10:29 55
- 13:17 57

2 Peter
- 1:19 40

1 John
- 1:1 6
- 1:7 55
- 5:11 12

Further reading on Andrew Fuller

Paul Brewster, *Andrew Fuller: Model Pastor-Theologian* (Studies in Baptist Life and Thought; Nashville, TN: B&H, 2010).

Andrew Gunton Fuller, *Andrew Fuller* (London: Hodder & Stoughton, 1882).

Keith S. Grant, *Andrew Fuller and the Evangelical Renewal of Pastoral Theology* (Studies in Baptist History and Thought, vol. 36; Milton Keynes, England: Paternoster, 2013).

Michael A.G. Haykin, *One heart and one soul: John Sutcliff of Olney, his friends, and his times* (Darlington, Co. Durham: Evangelical Press, 1994).

Michael A.G. Haykin, ed. *'At the Pure Fountain of Thy Word': Andrew Fuller as an Apologist* (Studies in Baptist History and Thought, vol. 6; Carlisle, Cumbria, UK/Waynesboro, GA: Paternoster Press, 2004).

Gilbert Laws, *Andrew Fuller, Pastor, Theologian, Ropeholder* (London: Carey Press, 1942).

Peter Morden, *Offering Christ to the World: Andrew Fuller (1754–1815) and the Revival of Eighteenth Century Particular Baptist Life* (Studies in Baptist History and Thought, vol. 8; Carlisle: Paternoster Press, 2003).

OTHER FULLER PUBLICATIONS BY H&E PUBLISHING

ISBN: 978-1-77526-334-0

Fuller deals with the issue of backsliding: when genuine Christians lose their passion for Christ and his kingdom. This was not a theoretical issue for Fuller, therefore, and his words, weighty when he first wrote them, are still worthy of being pondered—and acted upon.

ISBN: 978-1-7752633-5-7

Fuller believed that there was such a thing as truth, and that it could be known. His essay is thus a primer of what he calls "evangelical truth." Here he lays out what is the truth about the present state of humanity, that is, their fallenness, and the sole remedy for that state, namely, faith in the crucified and risen Christ as Lord.

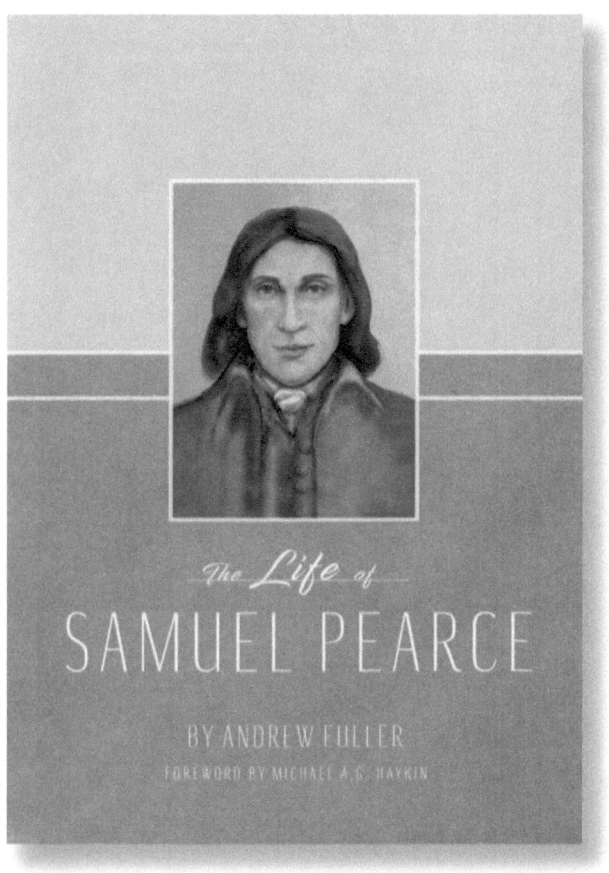

ISBN: 978-1-77526-339-5

In the eyes of Fuller, Samuel Pearce (1766–1799) was the epitome of the spirituality of their community. In fact, in that far-off day of the late eighteenth century Pearce was indeed well known for the anointing that attended his preaching and for the depth of his spirituality. It was said of him that "his ardour ... gave him a kind of ubiquity; as a man and a preacher, he was known, he was felt everywhere."

Date Completed	Name

H&E *Publishing*

WWW.HESEDANDEMET.COM

IN PARTNERSHIP WITH

Andrew Fuller
CENTER *for* BAPTIST STUDIES
at THE SOUTHERN BAPTIST THEOLOGICAL SEMINARY

www.andrewfullercenter.org

OTHER PUBLICATIONS BY H&E

John Bunyan, *Saved By Grace*

Matthew Henry, *A Church in the House*

Samuel Pearce, *Selected Works*

J.C. Ryle, *Baxter*

J.C. Ryle, *Latimer*

J.C. Ryle, *Whitefield*

About H&E Publishing

H&E Publishing is a Canadian evangelical publishing company located out of Peterborough, Ontario. We exist to provide Christ-exalting, Gospel-centred, and Bible-saturated content aimed to show God to be as glorious and worthy as He truly is.

We seek to provide rich resources that will equip, nourish, and refresh the Christian's soul. We desire to make available a variety of works that serve this purpose in the church. One key area of focus is to revive evangelicals of the past through updated reprints.

About

Andrew Fuller
CENTER *for* BAPTIST STUDIES
at THE SOUTHERN BAPTIST THEOLOGICAL SEMINARY

The Andrew Fuller Center for Baptist Studies, located at The Southern Baptist Theological Seminary in Louisville, Kentucky, seeks to promote the study of Baptist history as well as theological reflection on the contemporary significance of that history. The center is named in honor of Andrew Fuller (1754–1815), the late eighteenth- and early nineteenth- century English Baptist pastor and theologian, who played a key role in opposing aberrant thought in his day as well as being instrumental in the founding and early years of the Baptist Missionary Society.

Notes:

Notes:

Notes:

Notes:

Notes:

Notes:

Notes:

Notes:

Notes:

Notes:

Notes:

Notes:

Notes:

Notes:

Notes:

Notes:

Notes:

www.ingramcontent.com/pod-product-compliance
Lightning Source LLC
Chambersburg PA
CBHW020912080526
44589CB00011B/568